Georgia, My State
Biographies

Martin Luther King, Jr.

by Jill Ward

STATE
STANDARDS
PUBLISHING®

Your State • Your Standards • Your Grade Level

Dear Educators, Librarians and Parents . . .

Thank you for choosing the *"Georgia, My State" Biographies* series! We have designed this series to support the Georgia Department of Education's Georgia Performance Standards for second grade social studies. Each book in the series has been written at appropriate grade level as measured by the ATOS Readability Formula for Books (Accelerated Reader), the Lexile Framework for Reading, and the Fountas & Pinnell Benchmark Assessment System for Guided Reading, and has been evaluated by a reading program consultant to ensure grade-level appropriateness. Photographs and/or illustrations, captions, time line and other design elements have been included to provide supportive visual messaging to enhance text comprehension. Glossary and Word Index sections introduce key new words and help young readers develop skills in locating and combining information. A reproducible Teacher's Guide, available separately, provides opportunities for expanded supervised learning experiences. We wish you all success in using the *"Georgia, My State" Biographies* series to meet your student or child's learning needs. For additional sources of information, see www.georgiaencyclopedia.org and www.thekingcenter.org.

Jill Ward, President

Publisher
State Standards Publishing, LLC
5157 Hwy. 219, Suite 5
Fortson, GA 31808
USA
1.866.740.3056
www.statestandardspublishing.com

Library of Congress Cataloging-in-Publication Data
Ward, Jill, 1952-
  Martin Luther King, Jr. / by Jill Ward.
    p. cm. -- (Georgia, my state biographies)
  Includes bibliographical references and index.
  ISBN-13: 978-1-935077-01-5 (hardcover)
  ISBN-10: 1-935077-01-5 (hardcover)
  ISBN-13: 978-1-935077-08-4 (pbk.)
  ISBN-10: 1-935077-08-2 (pbk.)
    1.   King,   Martin   Luther,   Jr.,   1929-1968--Juvenile   literature.   2.
  African Americans--Biography--Juvenile literature. 3. Civil rights workers--United States--Biography--Juvenile literature. 4. Baptists--United States--Clergy--Biography--Juvenile literature. 5. African Americans--Civil rights--History--20th century--Juvenile literature. I. Title.
  E185.97.K5W28 2008
  323.092--dc22
  [B]   2008028939

Published in the United States of America.

Table of Contents

Martin was a pastor like his father and grandfather.

Martin Luther King, Jr.

Martin Luther King, Jr. was born in 1929 in Atlanta, Georgia. His father and his grandfather were church **pastors**. They taught the people about God.

Martin graduated from Morehouse College.

MOREHOUSE COLLEGE
FOUNDED 1867

DONATED BY
MOREHOUSE WOMEN'S
AUXILIARY
1973

TimeLine

1929
Born

1944
Starts college at 15

Martin was very smart. He went to Morehouse College in Atlanta. Martin went to college two years early. He was only 15 years old.

Martin was the best student in his class at the seminary.

TimeLine

1929	1944	1951 Graduates
Born	Starts college at 15	from seminary

Martin went to a **seminary** school after college. He learned to be a church pastor like his father and grandfather. Martin was the class President. He was also the class **valedictorian**. He had the highest grades in his graduating class. Martin got an award as the most out-standing student in his class.

TimeLine

1929
Born

1944
Starts college at 15

1951 Graduates
from seminary

1954 Moves to
Montgomery

A Civil Rights Problem

Martin married Coretta Scott after he graduated. They moved to Montgomery, Alabama. He was a church pastor. He saw that black people did not have the same **civil rights** as white people. They had to give up their seats on the bus for white people.

Martin told black people not to ride the bus.

Time Line

1929
Born

1944
Starts college at 15

1951 Graduates
from seminary

1954 Moves to
Montgomery

12

Martin Speaks Up

One day, a black woman named Rosa Parks would not give up her seat on the bus. She was put in jail. Martin spoke up for Rosa. He told black people to **boycott** the city buses. He told them not to ride them anymore. The boycott lasted a year. The buses were half empty.

Martin spoke up for the people. He was put in jail.

TimeLine

1929 Born

1944 Starts college at 15

1951 Graduates from seminary

1954 Moves to Montgomery

Martin kept speaking up for the people. He was put in jail many times for speaking. But Martin would not stop.

TimeLine

1929
Born

1944
Starts college at 15

1951 Graduates
from seminary

1954 Moves to
Montgomery

Martin made a speech in Washington, D. C. It is known as the "I Have a Dream" speech. He dreamed about black people and white people living together as equals. He dreamed they would have the same civil rights.

TimeLine

1929
Born

1944
Starts college at 15

1951 Graduates
from seminary

1954 Moves to
Montgomery

Learning To Make Peace

Martin became famous. Black people and white people listened to his speeches. He gave them hope of living together in peace. He won an award called the **Nobel Peace Prize**. It is given to people who solve important problems peacefully.

1955
Leads bus boycott

1963
Makes famous speech

1964
Gets Nobel Peace Prize

TimeLine

| 1929 Born | 1944 Starts college at 15 | 1951 Graduates from seminary | 1954 Moves to Montgomery |

Some people didn't agree with Martin. One man shot him. Martin died. He was only 39 years old. We remember Martin as the leader of the **Civil Rights Movement**. He fought for all people to have the same civil rights. We celebrate *Martin Luther King, Jr. Day* in January to remember Martin.

1955
Leads bus boycott

1963
Makes famous speech

1964
Gets Nobel Peace Prize

1969
Was killed

Glossary

boycott – choosing not to use or buy something to show that you disagree with what is being done.

civil rights – the benefits given to people who live in a free country. The right to vote and the right to eat in public restaurants are examples of civil rights benefits.

Civil Rights Movement – a time when people were speaking out to demand that black people be given the same civil rights as white people.

Nobel Peace Prize – a famous award given to people who work for peace.

pastors – people who lead a Christian church. Pastors teach people about God.

seminary – a school where people learn to be religious leaders, such as a pastor.

valedictorian – the person with the highest grades in a class that is graduating.

Word Index

Image Credits

About the Author

Jill Ward has more than twenty years' experience as a creative writer for business and organization promotional and educational needs, including video scripts, brochures, marketing and educational materials, white papers, and feature articles. She is the founder and President of State Standards Publishing and lives in Georgia with her husband, Harry.